A BOOK of NARNIANS

The LION, the WITCH and the OTHERS

C. S. LEWIS

A BOOK of
NARNIANS

The LION, the WITCH
and the OTHERS

Text Compiled by
JAMES RIORDAN

Illustrated by
PAULINE BAYNES

SCHOLASTIC INC.
New York Toronto London Auckland Sydney

Quotations throughout this book are taken from
The Chronicles of Narnia, written by C. S. Lewis:

THE MAGICIAN'S NEPHEW
THE LION, THE WITCH AND THE WARDROBE
THE HORSE AND HIS BOY
PRINCE CASPIAN
THE VOYAGE OF THE DAWN TREADER
THE SILVER CHAIR
THE LAST BATTLE

These quotations are used with the permission of C.S. Lewis (Pte) Limited.
"Narnia" is a trademark of C.S. Lewis (Pte) Limited.
"The Chronicles of Narnia" is a U.S. Registered Trademark of
C.S. Lewis (Pte) Limited.

ISBN 0-590-29211-0

Text copyright © 1994 by HarperCollins Publishers Ltd. and C.S. Lewis (Pte) Ltd.
Illustrations copyright © 1994 by HarperCollins Publishers Ltd.
All rights reserved. Published by Scholastic Inc., 555 Broadway, New York, NY 10012, by
arrangement with HarperCollins Publishers.

SCHOLASTIC and associated logos are trademarks and/or registered trademarks of
Scholastic Inc.

12 11 10 9 8 7 6 5 4 3 2 1   7 8 9/9 0 1 2/0

Printed in the U.S.A.   09
First Scholastic printing, October 1997

CONTENTS

FOREWORD

C.S. Lewis once wrote that the idea for the Narnia books came to him from images: "a faun carrying an umbrella, a queen in a sledge, a magnificent lion." From these mental pictures he created the Land of Narnia, a land populated with a rich diversity of beings, some very like their counterparts in our world, some derived from his knowledge and love of myth and fairy tale, and some, like Puddlegum, purely his own invention.

It is more than forty years since Pauline Baynes first gave shape to the creatures of Lewis's imagination. Her illustrations are loved throughout the world for their ability to convey the personalities of Lewis's characters as well as their physical appearance.

This book celebrates the inhabitants of Narnia, combining a text woven by James Riordan largely from Lewis's own words with Pauline Baynes's exquisitely detailed paintings.

Aslan

IN the darkness a voice began to sing. Its lower notes were deep enough to be the voice of the earth herself. It was the most beautiful sound one could ever hear. Far away, down near the horizon, the eastern sky changed from white to pink and from pink to gold. The Voice rose and rose, till all the air was shaking with it. And just as it swelled to the mightiest and most glorious sound it had yet produced, the sun arose.

You could imagine that the sun laughed for joy as it came up. And as its beams shot across the land, they lit up a valley through which a broad, swift river wound its way, flowing eastward toward the sun. It was a valley of mere earth, rock and water; there was not a tree, not a bush, not a blade of grass to be seen. The earth was of many colors: they were fresh, hot and vivid. They made you feel excited, until you saw the Singer himself, and then you forgot everything else.

IT was a Lion. Huge, shaggy and bright, it stood facing the risen sun. Its mouth was wide open in song and it was pacing to and fro about the empty land. And as Aslan walked and sang, the valley grew green with grass. It spread out from the Lion like a pool. It ran up the sides of the little hills like a wave.

In a few minutes it was creeping up the lower slopes of the distant mountains, making that young world every moment softer. A light wind could now be heard ruffling the grass which was sprinkled with daisies and buttercups. Along the river bank, willows were growing; on the other side, tangles of flowering currant, lilac, wild rose and rhododendron closed them in.

All this time the Lion's song and his stately prowl, to and fro, backward and forward, continued. It was clear that all the things were coming "out of the Lion's head." When you listened to his song you heard the things he was making up; and when you looked around you, you saw them all. This was Aslan's world of Narnia.

ASLAN

The White Witch

THE long gloomy hall was full of pillars and stone statues. There was a dwarf and the great shape of a centaur; and in the middle was a little faun with a sad expression on his face. The hall was guarded by a huge gray wolf, with hair bristling all along its back and a great red mouth. It was Maugrim, Chief of the Witch's Secret Police.

The only light came from a single lamp and close beside this sat the White Witch, who had put a spell on Narnia so that it was always winter and never Christmas. She was taller than any woman you have ever seen; she was covered in white fur up to her throat and she held a long golden wand and wore a golden crown on her head. Her face was white—like snow or paper or icing-sugar, except for her very red mouth. It was a beautiful face in other respects, but proud and cold and stern.

Fauns Dancing

ON fine nights when the cold and the drumtaps and the hooting of the owls and the moonlight get into their wild woodland blood, the fauns dance till daylight. The wild music, intensely sweet and just the slightest bit eerie too, is full of magic; but of the good kind, not like a witch's thrumming.

To faint drumming and a wild and dreamy tune, many light feet foot it around the Dancing Lawn, covering the grass with little cloven hoof-marks. Some play reedy pipes, some have leaf-crowned heads, but all take part in the dance with so many complicated steps and figures it would take an onlooker some time to understand it.

The fauns are not much taller than dwarfs, but far slighter and more graceful. From the waist upward they are like men, but glossy black hair covers their legs, and their feet are those of goats. They also have long tufted tails. Many of them have short pointed beards and curly brown hair, and out of the hair stick two little horns, one on each side of the forehead. Their skin is reddish and the upper part of their bodies gleams naked in the pale light as they dance. Among the strange but pleasant faces, which seem mournful and merry all at once, there are Mentius, Dumnus and Girbius, Voluns and Voltinus, Nimienus and Nausus, Oscuns and Obentinus.

The Beavers

THERE was a dam with ice frozen into foamy, wavy shapes, and a glittering wall of icicles, as if the side of the dam had been covered all over by flowers and wreaths and festoons of purest sugar. On top of the dam was a funny little house shaped like an enormous beehive, and from a hole in the roof came smoke.

A whiskered, furry face was peering down into a little hole in the ice. It was Mr. Beaver fishing. Suddenly he shot out a wrinkled old paw and whisked out a beautiful trout; then he did it all over again until he had a fine catch of fish.

These he took into the snug little house.

Mrs. Beaver popped the trout into a sizzling frying pan. There's nothing to beat good freshwater fish if you eat it when it has been alive half an hour ago and has come out of the pan half a minute ago.

Trees

ALL the trees of the world appeared to be rushing to greet Aslan, bowing and curtseying and waving thin long arms. Pale birch-girls were tossing their heads, willow-women pushed back their hair from their brooding faces, the queenly beeches stood still and adored him, shaggy oak-men, lean and melancholy elms, shock-headed hollies (dark themselves, but their wives all bright with berries) and gay rowans, all bowed and rose again, shouting, "Aslan, Aslan!" in their various husky or creaking or wavelike voices.

Dufflepuds

THE Duffers were dwarfs who were "uglified" into one-legged Monopods by the Magician after they had defied him. They made themselves invisible because they could not bear to look at one another. So stupid were they that they washed up plates and knives *before* dinner to save time afterward; and they planted boiled potatoes to save cooking them when they were dug up.

The Monopods had a single thick leg under which was an enormous broad-toed foot with toes curling up. They loved to use their foot as a boat on water, paddling about like a fleet of little canoes, with a dwarf in the stern.

They moved about by jumping like fleas or frogs. And what jumps they made!—as if each big foot were a mass of springs. And with what a bounce they came down, thumpety-thump, upon the ground. They would sleep, like mushrooms, with their single three-foot foot up in the air like an umbrella.

They finally became visible; but they mixed up their old name Duffers with Monopods and called themselves Dufflepuds.

Tash

IN the shadow of the trees something was moving. At first glance you might have mistaken it for smoke, for it was gray and you could see things through it. But the deathly smell was not the smell of smoke. And it kept its shape instead of billowing and curling like smoke. It was the shape of a man, but it had the head of some bird of prey with a cruel, curved beak.

It had four arms which it held high above its head, stretching them out northward as if it wanted to snatch all Narnia in its grip; and its fingers—all twenty of them—were curved like its beak and had long, pointed, birdlike claws instead of nails. It floated on the grass instead of walking, and the grass seemed to wither beneath it.

This was Tash! Tash, the false or demon god of the Calormenes, the destroyer of Narnia.

Bacchus, Silenus and the River-god

BACCHUS was dressed only in a fawn-skin, with vine leaves wreathed in his curly hair. Old, fat Silenus came riding on a donkey, shouting:

"Refreshments! Euan, euan, eu-oi-oi-oi."

And all the time there were more and more vines and grapes everywhere; the donkey was a mass of them.

Then up out of a pool came a great wet, bearded head, crowned with rushes. It was the river-god. Trunks of ivy came curling up, growing as quickly as fire grows.

The wild romp continued, the laughter never ceased, nor the yodeling cries of "Euan, euan, eu-oi-oi-oi-oi."

Doctor Cornelius

DOCTOR Cornelius, the new tutor, was the smallest and fattest man you could ever see. He had a long, silvery, pointed beard, and his face looked very wise, very ugly and very kind.

One night, muffled in a hooded robe, he took his pupil up the dark, winding stair of the castle to the tower roof. There was no difficulty in picking out the two stars they had come to see. They hung low in the sky, almost as bright as two little moons and very close together.

"Are they going to have a collision?" asked his pupil.

"Nay, dear Prince," said Doctor Cornelius. "The great lords of the upper sky know the steps of their dance too well for that. Their meeting is fortunate and means some great good for the sad realm of Narnia. Tarva, the Lord of Victory, salutes Alambil, the Lady of Peace."

Shasta and Aravis

WITH a Talking Horse, the orphan Shasta escaped to Narnia. The old war horse's name was Breehy-hinny-brinny-hoohy-hah—Bree for short. After riding for several weeks, they were crossing a wide plain when they noticed another rider and horse behind them. Shasta and Bree discovered that their companions were a girl called Aravis and a Talking Horse, Hwin; they too were running away and, together, the children and the horses continued their journey to Narnia.

Just ahead of them was a smooth green wall in the middle of which was an open gate guarded by a tall bearded man in a robe colored like autumn leaves. Before they could reach safety, however, they heard a long snarling roar and saw a huge tawny lion, its body low to the ground, gaining on the second horse. Shasta saw the lion rise up on its hind legs and its terrible claws tear at the mare's back. Then, to his relief, the lion turned head over heels and rushed away.

Trufflehunter

PRINCE Caspian was lying on a bed of heather in a firelit cave. He felt an arm slip under his shoulders and a cup of something sweet and hot set to his lips. The face before him was very hairy and very long nosed. It was larger and friendlier and more intelligent than the face of any creature he had ever seen before. It was Trufflehunter the Badger.

Jewel

NO man can match a Unicorn in battle, for it rears on its hind legs as it falls upon you and then you have its hoofs and its horn and its teeth to deal with all at once. Jewel the Unicorn was tossing men as you'd toss hay on a fork. Its head came down and, next moment, the enemy lay dead, gored through the heart by Jewel's horn.

Giants of Harfang

THE travelers suddenly saw a castle on a high crag and lights. Not moonlight, nor fires, but homely, cheering rows of lighted windows. It was Harfang, home of the Harfang Giants. Numb with cold, Jill, Puddleglum and Eustace battled through the snowstorm, thinking of great halls with fires roaring on the hearth and hot soup and juicy sirloins on the table.

The first giant they met was taller than an apple tree. "Come in, little shrimps!" he said. They were shown into the throne room where the giants were all in magnificent robes. Puddleglum collapsed on the floor: with his long limbs, he looked just like a large spider.

The King had a fine, curled beard and a straight eaglelike nose; but the Queen was dreadfully fat. She took pity on Jill who had begun to cry as the fire's warmth made her frozen ears tingle.

"They're dear little things at that age," murmured one giantess. "It seems almost a pity . . ." Though the children did not know it, the giants intended to turn them into man-pies and eat them.

The Sea People

SHAFTS of sunlight fell through the blue waves upon a green wooded valley. A hunting party of Sea People was riding along on olive-green sea horses. Each man and woman wore a crown and pearls; gold gleamed on their foreheads below purple hair, and emerald or orange streamers fluttered from their shoulders. Their bodies were the color of old ivory.

The riders had long, cruel spears in their hands and a fierce blue fish on their wrists; this they released as they chased shoals of fat fish. Glittering in the sunlight was a castle city, nestling upon a high mountain. The city was knobbly and jagged and of a pearly-ivory hue.

Beware! For amid the light, the silence, the tingling smell of the Silver Sea, woe betide the sailor who gazes for long upon the lovely People of the Sea.

Eustace the Dragon

EUSTACE Scrubb was a selfish brat. One day he found treasure in a dragon's lair beside a pool—crowns, coins, rings, bracelets, plates and gems. And he fell asleep. When he awoke, he saw two thin columns of smoke curling up before his eyes, black against the moonlight. Staring into the pool, he was horrified to see a long, green snout, dull red eyes, a long scaly body, cruel claws, huge bat's wings and yards of tail.

He had turned into a dragon while asleep. Sleeping on a dragon's hoard with greedy, dragonish thoughts in his heart, he had become a dragon himself. Eustace the Dragon began to cry. A powerful dragon crying its eyes out under the moon in a deserted valley is a rare sight and sound indeed!

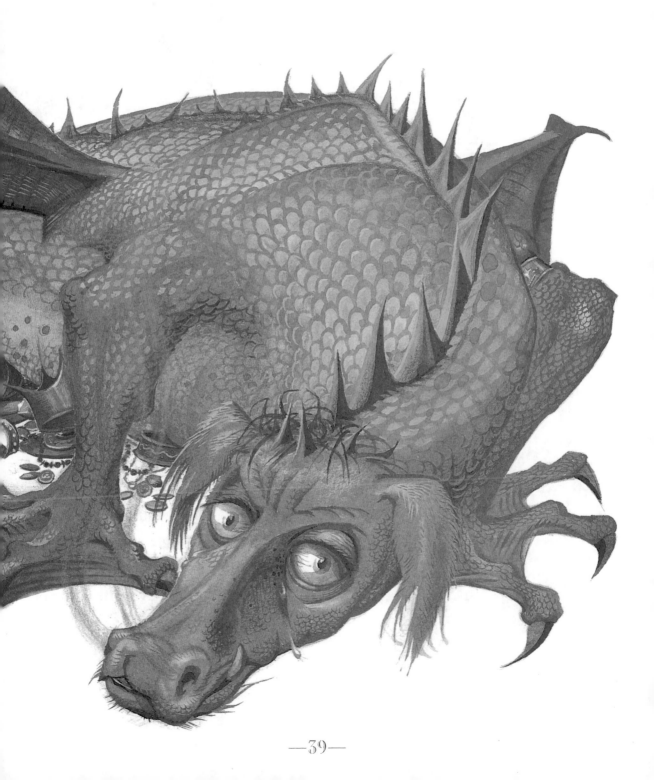

Seven Brothers of Shuddering Wood

PRINCE Caspian, Trumpkin the Red Dwarf and Nikabrik the Black Dwarf were taken by a dwarf to the bottom of a dark stairway and into a smithy lit up by a furnace. Two Red Dwarfs were at the bellows, another was holding a piece of red-hot metal on the anvil with a pair of tongs, a fourth was hammering it, and two, wiping their horny little hands on a greasy cloth, came forward to meet the visitors.

They were the Seven Brothers of Shuddering Wood.

Their gifts were noble—mail

shirts and helmets and swords; the workmanship was finer than any Caspian had ever seen.

Narnian Dwarfs, though less than four feet high, are the toughest and strongest creatures there are. Some are evil, like the Witch's servant, a fat Dwarf dressed in polar bear's fur and a red hood with a long gold tassel; his huge beard covered his knees like a rug. It was he who handed Edmund a jeweled cup full of a foamy, steamy drink. Trumpkin and Poggin, with his spade and lantern, are good and helpful Dwarfs. But most, like Griffle, black bearded, with a pick and lantern, are ever suspicious and believe the opposite of what they are told.

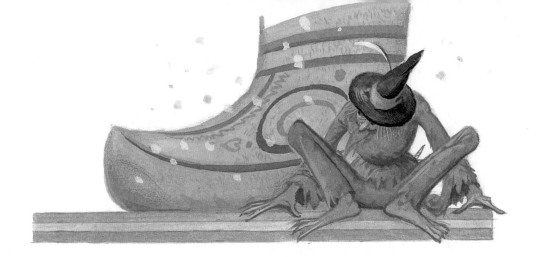

Puddleglum

PUDDLEGLUM was a Marsh-wiggle who lived in a wigwam in the center of a flat marsh covered with coarse grass.

Like the marsh, he was a sort of muddy-brown color. He had a long, thin face with sunken cheeks, a tightly shut mouth and no beard. His straggly hair was greeny-gray, like reeds or rushes, and he wore a high, pointed hat like a steeple, with an enormously wide brim.

From a distance he seemed all arms and legs, so that when he sat down he looked uncommonly like a large spider. Yet the fingers of his hands were webbed like a frog's, and so were his bare feet which dangled in the muddy water. He was dressed in earth-colored clothes that hung loose about him.

Marsh-wiggles smoke a very strange, heavy sort of tobacco (some folk say they mix it with mud); the smoke from their pipe trickles out of the bowl and drifts along the ground like black-gray mist. Their expressions are solemn, so that you can see at once they take a serious view of life.

The Centaurs

HALF-man, half-horse, the Centaurs canter through the Narnian woods. The horse part of them is like huge English farm horses, the man part is like stern but beautiful giants, some with golden beards flowing over their magnificent bare chests.

They are solemn, majestic people, full of ancient wisdom; they are not easily made either merry or angry, but their anger is as terrible as a tidal wave when it comes.

The Giants

GIANTS are not at all clever. Poor Wimbleweather of Deadman's Hill, though as brave as a lion, would burst into one of those not very intelligent laughs to which the nicer sort of Giants are so liable, then he would check himself and look as grave as a turnip. One time he carried on his back a basketful of rather seasick Dwarfs who had accepted his offer of a lift and were wishing they had walked instead.

When Aslan breathed on the stone statues in the Witch's castle, he started with Giant Rumblebuffin's feet: life crept up his legs and, a moment later, he lifted his club off his shoulder, rubbed his eyes and said, "Bless me! I must have been asleep." And he beamed all over his ugly honest face.

Mr. Tumnus

MR. Tumnus carried over his head an umbrella, white with snow. From the waist upward he was a man, but his legs were shaped like a goat's and instead of feet he had goat's hoofs. He also had a tail which was neatly caught up over his free arm so as to keep it from trailing in the snow.

He had a red woolen muffler around his neck and his skin was rather reddish too. All about him the snowy ground was rough and there were rocks with little hills up and little hills down. At the bottom of a small valley was a cave of reddish stone. This was his house: it might not look much on the outside, but inside it was warm and cozy.

Soon afterward Tumnus the Faun was turned to stone in the White Witch's castle—for helping Lucy. But when Aslan breathed on him he came back to life. A moment later Lucy and Mr. Tumnus were holding each other by both hands and dancing around for joy. The little chap was none the worse for having been a statue.

Wer-Wolf and Hag

THE Wer-Wolf was a horrible, gray, gaunt beast, half-man, half-wolf. The Hag's nose and chin stuck out like a pair of nutcrackers, and her dirty gray hair flew about her face as she pounced on her victims.

The Three Bulgy Bears

PRINCE Caspian tapped three times on the trunk of an old hollow oak tree and a woolly sort of voice from inside said, "Go away. It's not time to get up yet."

When he tapped again, there was a noise like a small earthquake and a sort of door opened and out came three brown bears, very bulgy indeed and blinking their little eyes. When everything had been explained to them, they kissed Caspian—very wet, snuffly kisses they were—and offered him some honey.

Trumpkin

TRUMPKIN, the Red Dwarf, was very stocky and deep-chested, like most dwarfs. He was about three feet high when standing up, and he had an immense beard and whiskers of coarse red hair which left little of his face to be seen except a beaklike nose and twinkling black eyes. He smoked a pipe about the size of his own arm, blowing out great clouds of fragrant smoke. Now and again, he would mutter odd words, like "Beards and bedsteads!" "Bulbs and bolsters!" and "Soup and celery!"

Trumpkin accompanied Prince Caspian to Aslan's How. It was an awesome place, a round green hill on top of another hill, long since overgrown with trees, with one little, low doorway leading into it. The tunnels inside were a perfect maze, and they were lined and roofed with smooth stones on which were strange characters and snaky patterns, and pictures in which the form of a lion was repeated again and again. It all seemed to belong to an even older Narnia than the Narnia they all knew.

Animal Characters

"CREATURES, I give you yourselves," said Aslan. "I give you forever this land of Narnia." So the animals became Talking Beasts and were warned not to go back to their old ways.

Thereafter, the Talking Beasts were mostly good. The red-chested, bright-eyed Robin guided the children through the wood. Camillo the Hare, Hogglestock the Hedgehog and Clodsley Shovel the Mole all helped Prince Caspian to save Narnia. And Farsight the Eagle fought bravely in the last battle for Narnia, flying at enemy faces and pecking at their eyes. Pattertwig the red Squirrel was full of courage and energy and mischief.

The wisest of the beasts was Glimfeather, a white Owl so big it stood as high as a good-sized dwarf. It was Glimfeather who carried Jill on its back through the cool, damp night air to the parliament of owls in a ruined, fusty tower; there they told her: "Tu-whoo. Tu-whoo. That's the right thing to do."

Most helpful of all were the mice—the nibblers and gnawers and nutcrackers; these sharp-

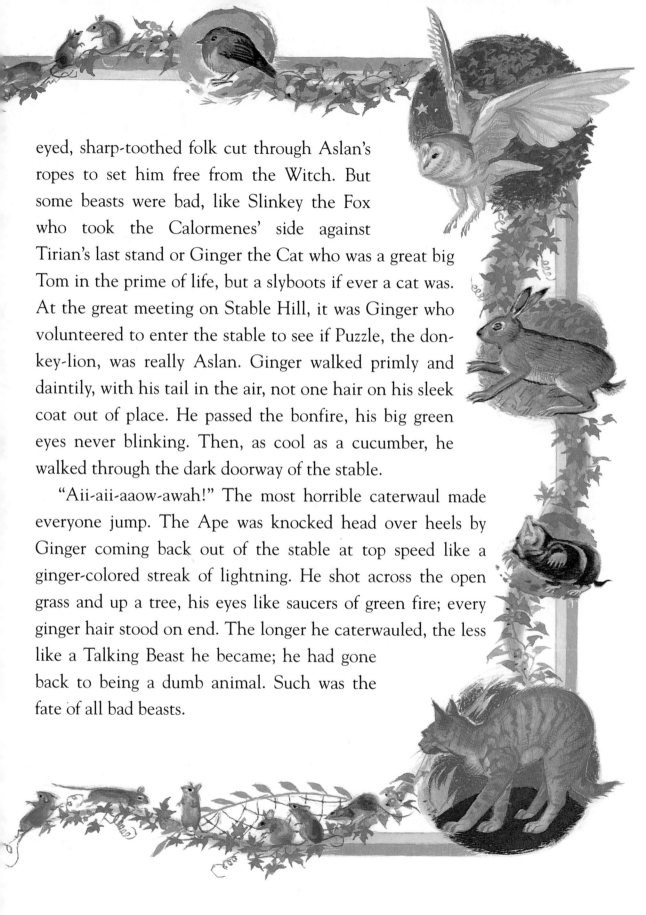

eyed, sharp-toothed folk cut through Aslan's ropes to set him free from the Witch. But some beasts were bad, like Slinkey the Fox who took the Calormenes' side against Tirian's last stand or Ginger the Cat who was a great big Tom in the prime of life, but a slyboots if ever a cat was. At the great meeting on Stable Hill, it was Ginger who volunteered to enter the stable to see if Puzzle, the donkey-lion, was really Aslan. Ginger walked primly and daintily, with his tail in the air, not one hair on his sleek coat out of place. He passed the bonfire, his big green eyes never blinking. Then, as cool as a cucumber, he walked through the dark doorway of the stable.

"Aii-aii-aaow-awah!" The most horrible caterwaul made everyone jump. The Ape was knocked head over heels by Ginger coming back out of the stable at top speed like a ginger-colored streak of lightning. He shot across the open grass and up a tree, his eyes like saucers of green fire; every ginger hair stood on end. The longer he caterwauled, the less like a Talking Beast he became; he had gone back to being a dumb animal. Such was the fate of all bad beasts.

Shift

SHIFT was the craftiest, ugliest, most wrinkled Ape you can imagine. One day he found a tattered, slimy lion's skin in Caldron Pool—the big dancing, bubbling, churning pool into which pours the great waterfall with a noise like everlasting thunder.

Shift scrambled down from his thatched house in the fork of a tree: he had a ball of thread in his mouth, a needle between his lips and scissors in his paw. He intended to sew a beautiful new lion-skin coat.

Reepicheep

REEPICHEEP was well over a foot high when he stood on his hind legs, with ears nearly as long as a rabbit's. He wore a tiny rapier at his side and was forever twirling his long whiskers as if they were a moustache. The sleek, bright-eyed Talking Mouse was one of the great heroes of Narnia who had fought at the fierce Battle of Beruna and afterward sailed to the World's End with King Caspian the Seafarer. When he was born, a wood woman had spoken a verse over his cradle; and he often sang it in his chirruping voice:

> *"Where sky and water meet,*
> *Where the waves grow sweet,*
> *Doubt not, Reepicheep,*
> *To find all you seek,*
> *There is the utter East."*

So when he reached the Silver Sea, he set off alone in his coracle, paddling through an endless carpet of lilies. For a split second he hovered on the crest of a wave and then was gone.

Fledge

FLEDGE spread his wings wider than angels' wings in church windows. The feathers shone chestnut and copper in the dazzling sunlight as he soared over Narnia, its many-colored lawns and rocks and heather spread out below, its river winding through the land like a ribbon of quicksilver.

Once he had been a common cab horse called Strawberry, son of a cavalry officer's charger. Now he was Fledge, father of all flying horses.

Earthmen

THE Earthmen in the Deep Realm were padding through the cavern lit with a cold gray-blue light. The dense crowd contained all shapes and sizes, from little gnomes barely a foot high to stately figures taller than men. Some had tails, some wore big beards and others had round, smooth faces as big as pumpkins. Several had horns in the middle of their foreheads.

But in some respects they were all alike: every face was as long as a fiddle, all carried three-pronged spears and all were dreadfully pale. Beware: for many fall into Underland, but few return to the sunlit lands.

Puzzle

PUZZLE the donkey was rather fat with a soft, gray coat and a gentle, honest face. Because he was so trusting, he let the crafty Ape, Shift, dress him in a lion's skin and make out he was the great Aslan. Shift would only bring him out of his stable at night to show to the Narnians—who could not see his silly, donkeyish face in the dark.

So the Narnians carried out his orders, unsuspecting that they really came from the evil Shift.

It was Jill who discovered the truth: one dark night she went to Stable Hill and, by the light of a great bonfire, she saw the donkey-lion. The real Aslan finally appeared and pardoned Puzzle the donkey who said how sorry he was.

Maenads and the Minotaur

AT midnight the dancing began. The Naiads who lived in the wells, the Dryads who lived in the trees and the Maenads, fierce madcap girls, came out to dance with the Minotaur. It was rather like Blind Man's Buff, as everyone behaved as if they were blindfolded; it was not unlike Hunt the Slipper, though the slipper was never found.

Everyone began eating; you have never tasted such grapes. Really good grapes, bursting into cool sweetness when you put them into your mouth.

Here, there was more than anyone could possibly want, and no table manners at all. One saw sticky and stained

fingers everywhere, and, though mouths were full, the laughter never ceased, nor the yodeling shouts, till all of a sudden everyone felt that the game and the feast ought to be over; and they all flopped down breathless on the ground.

At that moment the sun was rising and the wild girls all vanished into the trees.

Ghouls

THE White Witch summoned up all the evil spirits. She called out Ogres with monstrous teeth, Werwolves and Bull-headed men, Ghouls and Boggles, Cruels and Hags and Horrors, Efreets and Sprites and Orknies, Wooses and Ettins, people of the Toadstools and Poison Plants. All were grinning and leering, dancing up and down in the moonlight; some carried torches burning with red flames and black smoke.

Dryads

THE whole forest was coming awake. The birches became slender girls dressed in silver, with hair blown about their faces; their voices were so soft and showery the nightingale stopped singing as if to listen to their song. Larch-girls were dressed in green so bright it was almost yellow, with ivy curling round them, growing as quickly as fire grows.

The oak was a hearty old man with a frizzled beard and warts on his face and hands, and hair growing out of the warts. Beech-girls, dressed in fresh, transparent green, were the best of all: for they were gracious goddesses, smooth and stately, the ladies of the wood.

Dwarfs

Aglorious feast appeared before the Dwarfs: pies, tongues, pigeons, trifles, ices, and a goblet of good red wine. They began eating and drinking greedily; yet very soon the Dwarfs began suspecting each other of finding something nicer, and they started grabbing and snatching, and went on quarreling and very soon all the good food was smeared on their faces and clothes or trodden underfoot.

The Dwarfs work very hard: they ply their picks and spades to the snowy hillside even on the rawest nights. With a fire blazing, bellows roaring, hammers clinking on the anvil, they shape gold into the finest crowns.

"Wrong will be right, when Aslan comes in sight,
    At the sound of his roar, sorrows will be no more,
    When he bares his teeth, winter meets its death,
    And when he shakes his mane, we shall have spring again."

CAST OF CHARACTERS

ARAVIS is a young girl who escapes from the realm of Calormen on her Talking Horse Hwin and meets up with Shasta and Bree. While Aravis features mainly in *The Horse and His Boy*, we meet her again in *The Last Battle*, by which time she has married Shasta, now King Cor, and become Queen of Archenland.

ASLAN is the Great Lion and adversary of the White Witch; he calls Narnia to life, dies for its people, but comes back to life and triumphs over the White Witch. Aslan first appears in *The Magician's Nephew*, singing his great creation of Narnia song; he meets Peter, Edmund, Lucy and Susan in *The Lion, the Witch and the Wardrobe*, sacrifices his life to save Edmund, but revives to defeat the White Witch and crown the children Kings and Queens of Narnia. In *The Horse and His Boy*, Aslan protects Shasta and helps him save Archenland; and in *Prince Caspian*, he reawakens Narnia and makes Caspian King. Aslan turns himself into an albatross and a lamb in *The Voyage of the* Dawn Treader, while in *The Silver Chair* he rescues Eustace and brings Caspian into True life in Aslan's country. Aslan returns to Narnia in *The Last Battle* to lead the Narnians into the real Narnia.

BACCHUS is the god of wine who inspires song, dance and revelry. He makes a brief appearance in *The Lion, the Witch and the Wardrobe* and *Prince Caspian*.

BEAVERS are helpful creatures who live in a beehive-shaped house on a dam. They are to be found in *The Lion, the Witch and the Wardrobe*.

BLACK DWARFS are usually, but not necessarily, wicked servants of the White Witch. They do their evil deeds in *The Last Battle*.

BREE is a Talking Horse who was kidnapped from Narnia. He takes Shasta from the land of Calormen to Narnia in *The Horse and His Boy* and also appears briefly in *The Last Battle*.

BULGY BEARS are three slow-moving, slow-witted bears who help Prince Caspian in *Prince Caspian*.

CALORMENES are the men of the kingdom of Calormen who fight against the Narnians in the last great battle. While they are the main foe in *The Last Battle*, they also appear as cruel merchants in *The Voyage of the* Dawn Treader, and it is their land of Calormen that provides the background to *The Horse and His Boy*.

CAMILLO is a Hare who helps Caspian save Narnia in *Prince Caspian*.

CASPIAN is a Prince of Telmarine blood who defeats his usurping uncle to become the rightful King of Narnia. Caspian's adventures are related in *Prince Caspian* and *The Voyage of the* Dawn Treader. In *The Silver Chair*, he dies and then is revived in Aslan's land, where he also appears briefly at the end of *The Last Battle*.

CENTAURS are half-man, half-horse. These wise, majestic beasts roam the Narnian woods. They gallop through several books, giving wise counsel in *The Lion, the Witch and the Wardrobe*, *The Horse and His Boy*, *Prince Caspian* and *The Silver Chair*.

CLODSEY SHOVEL is a Mole who helps Prince Caspian in *Prince Caspian*.

DOCTOR CORNELIUS is the half-dwarf tutor to Prince Caspian; he becomes Lord Chancellor when Caspian is made King of Narnia. He appears in *Prince Caspian*.

DRYADS are spirits of the trees and appear in *The Lion, the Witch and the Wardrobe*, *Prince Caspian*, *The Voyage of the* Dawn Treader, *The Silver Chair* and *The Last Battle*.

DUFFLEPUDS are rather stupid dwarfs, who were "uglified" by the Magician into one-legged Monopods in *The Voyage of the* Dawn Treader and used a spell to make themselves invisible because they could not bear to look at one another.

EARTHMEN are creatures who inhabit Underland. They are forced to work for the Witch and live a miserable life in the dark caves beneath the earth in *The Silver Chair*.

EUSTACE THE DRAGON is a boy who turns into a dragon because he is greedy and selfish in *The Voyage of the* Dawn Treader. He also features in *The Silver Chair*.

FARSIGHT is an eagle who fights bravely in the last battle for Narnia in *The Last Battle*.

FAUNS are half-man, half-goat. They dance all night to wild music on the Dancing Lawn and appear in all the books.

FLEDGE was once a common cab horse called Strawberry in *The Magician's Nephew* and turns into the flying horse Fledge; he also features as Fledge in *The Last Battle*.

GINGER is a sly tomcat who turns dumb after entering the stable to see if Puzzle is really Aslan in *The Last Battle*.

GLIMFEATHER is a white Owl as big as a Dwarf who bears Jill on his back to the owl parliament. He features mainly in *The Silver Chair*, but comes to the great meeting of all helpful animals in *The Last Battle*.

GRIFFLE is a black-bearded dwarf who, like many other Dwarfs, believes the opposite of what he is told. He appears in *The Last Battle*.

HAGS are young women who have sacrificed their youth and beauty for the ability to practice Black Magic. One Hag joins Nikabrik's scheme to call up the White Witch from the dead in *Prince Caspian* and is beheaded by Trumpkin's sword. Hags also appear as members of the White Witch's army in *The Lion, the Witch and the Wardrobe*.

HARFANG GIANTS are evil giants who live in Harfang Castle set upon a high crag in *The Silver Chair*.

HOGGLESTOCK is a Hedgehog who helps Prince Caspian in *Prince Caspian*.

HWIN is a Talking Horse who was stolen from Narnia by the Calormenes. She escapes with the girl Aravis back to the land of Narnia in *The Horse and His Boy*. She also makes a brief appearance in *The Last Battle*.

JEWEL is a Unicorn and companion of King Tirian; he fights bravely for Narnia in *The Last Battle*.

MAENADS are wild madcap girls who follow Bacchus and perform a magic dance of plenty in *Prince Caspian*.

MAUGRIM is also known as Fenris Ulf; a huge gray wolf, the Chief of the White Witch's Secret Police in *The Lion, the Witch and the Wardrobe*.

MINOTAUR is a creature half-man, half-bull in *The Lion, the Witch and the Wardrobe*.

NIKABRIK is a sour Black Dwarf who schemes to call up the White Witch from the dead in *Prince Caspian* and is killed when he and his evil companions attack the Prince and his friends.

PATTERTWIG is a red Squirrel, a chatterbox, but full of courage and energy, who appears in *Prince Caspian*.

POGGIN is a good, helpful Dwarf in *The Last Battle*.

PUDDLEGLUM is a Marsh-wiggle who lives in a wigwam in the center of a marsh; he accompanies Jill and Eustace on their adventures. Puddleglum features all the way through *The Silver Chair* and is present at the grand meeting in *The Last Battle*.

PUZZLE is a gentle, trusting donkey deceived by the crafty Ape Shift into pretending to be Aslan in *The Last Battle*.

RED DWARFS are sometimes helpful Dwarfs, like Trumpkin and Poggin, but can also be bad. They are to be found in *The Lion, the Witch and the Wardrobe*, *The Horse and His Boy*, *Prince Caspian* and *The Last Battle*.

REEPICHEEP is a Talking Mouse of Narnia who fights bravely at the great Battle of Beruna and afterward sails to the End of the World with King Caspian. He first makes an appearance in *Prince Caspian*; although he paddles off in *The Voyage of the Dawn Treader* and "since that moment no one can truly claim to have seen Reepicheep the Mouse," he does make a final appearance in *The Last Battle*.

RUMBLEBUFFIN is an honest, good-natured Giant who is trapped as a statue in the White Witch's fortress in *The Lion, the Witch and the Wardrobe*. He helps the prisoners escape from the fortress by breaking down the gates with his huge club.

RIVER-GOD emerges from the Great River at Beruna Bridge in *Prince Caspian* and is also mentioned in *The Magician's Nephew*.

SEA PEOPLE are beautiful creatures who live under the Silver Sea, riding olive-green sea horses and enticing unwary sailors to their doom in *The Voyage of the Dawn Treader*.

SEVEN BROTHERS OF SHUDDERING WOOD are seven Red Dwarfs. Prince Caspian visits their smithy in *Prince Caspian*.

SHASTA is an orphan boy who escapes an evil Tarkaan and rides the Talking Horse Bree to safety in Narnia. His adventures are related in *The Horse and His Boy*, and he reappears as King Cor of Archenland in *The Last Battle*.

SHIFT is a crafty Ape who tricks the Narnian animals into thinking that Puzzle, the donkey covered in a lion-skin, is really Aslan in *The Last Battle*.

SILENUS is a fat old man riding a donkey; tutor and foster father to Bacchus. He makes a short entry in both *The Lion, the Witch and the Wardrobe* and *Prince Caspian*.

SLINKEY is a fox who fights against King Tirian in *The Last Battle*.

TASH is vulture-headed demon, with four arms and claws instead of fingers. He is the god of the Calormenes and destroyer of Narnia in *The Last Battle*.

TIRIAN, KING, is the last of the Kings of Narnia in *The Last Battle*.

TRUFFLEHUNTER is a wise and friendly Badger who helps Caspian in *Prince Caspian*; he also makes a final appearance with all the helpful animals in *The Last Battle*.

TRUMPKIN is the Red Dwarf who accompanies Caspian to Aslan's How. He continues his helpful deeds from *Prince Caspian* to *The Voyage of the* Dawn Treader and *The Silver Chair*; and he turns up at the great meeting in *The Last Battle*.

TUMNUS is half-man, half-goat, a faun who helps Lucy against the White Witch, for which she turns him to stone. Aslan eventually brings him back to life. Mr. Tumnus first features early in The *Lion, the Witch and the Wardrobe*, as the Witch's spy who nonetheless helps Lucy; he further appears in *The Horse and His Boy* and *The Last Battle*.

WER-WOLF is a fearful gray beast, half-man, half-wolf, who appears in *Prince Caspian*.

WHITE WITCH is the evil witch who puts a spell on Narnia so that it is always winter; she is finally defeated by Aslan. She is initially Jadis, Queen of Charn, in *The Magician's Nephew*, and then becomes the evil Witch in *The Lion, the Witch and the Wardrobe*, where she kills Aslan with a stone knife; when Aslan comes back to life he finally destroys the Witch and her evil power, so ending the hundred years of winter. The White Witch reappears as the Green Lady/Queen of Underland in *The Silver Chair*.

WIMBLEWEATHER is a giant of Deadman's Hill; brave but dim, he fights for Caspian and Peter in *Prince Caspian*.

THE CHRONICLES OF NARNIA

THE MAGICIAN'S NEPHEW

Digory and Polly vanish to another world where they release the evil Queen Jadis from a prisoning spell. Jadis follows them back to their own world and creates total chaos until, by accident, they all find themselves in yet another world, a world where there is nothing but darkness. Aslan the Lion appears and the children listen to his song as he creates the enchanted land of Narnia.

THE LION, THE WITCH AND THE WARDROBE

Peter, Susan, Edmund and Lucy step through Professor Kirke's wardrobe into the land of Narnia where the White Witch's cruel hold has kept the land in perpetual winter. Edmund betrays his brother and sisters to the White Witch and leads her to them as they make their way toward the Stone Table to meet Aslan, the only one with the power to defeat the Witch and restore summer to Narnia.

THE HORSE AND HIS BOY

When Shasta learns that he is not Arsheesh the fisherman's son, he decides to escape from the cruel land of Calormen. With the help of the Talking Horse Bree and accompanied by Aravis, a fearless runaway girl, he goes north to find Narnia. Their journey is perilous but they finally reach Narnia where the air is sweet and there is freedom and happiness. Only then does Shasta discover who he really is.

PRINCE CASPIAN

Civil war is destroying Narnia. Prince Caspian, the rightful heir to the throne, resolves to restore the land to its original glory. A magic horn draws Lucy, Edmund, Peter and Susan back to Narnia to rally support for the young Prince and to fight for his cause. With the children's help and the aid of Aslan, Caspian fights to regain his kingdom so that animals, Dwarfs, trees and flowers can once again live in harmony.

THE VOYAGE OF THE DAWN TREADER

Lucy, Edmund and their unpleasant cousin Eustace enter a painting into the land of Narnia. On board the Dawn Treader they journey to the Eastern Islands with King Caspian and his crew in search of the seven lost friends of King Caspian's father. As they voyage toward the end of the world, they visit many strange islands and encounter magical creatures, but are never deterred from their quest.

THE SILVER CHAIR

Jill and Eustace escape from their dreadful school to Narnia where Aslan sends them on a mission to rescue Prince Rilian, heir to the old King of Narnia. Jill is given four signs by Aslan to help the children find the Prince. With Puddleglum the Marshwiggle to act as their guide, they journey to the Bottom of the World to try and free the prince from the Queen of Underland and the bindings of his silver chair.

THE LAST BATTLE

Narnia is in confusion as an impostor of Aslan threatens to corrupt the animals and destroy the harmony of the once glorious kingdom. King Tirian, the last King of Narnia, calls on Aslan and the helpers beyond the world for aid. Jill and Eustace appear and help gather the troops together. King Tirian challenges his enemies to fight and, in the light of a huge bonfire, the last and greatest battle of Narnia begins.

C. S. LEWIS'S OUTLINE OF NARNIAN HISTORY

NARNIAN YEARS

ENGLISH YEARS

1888 Digory Kirke born.
1889 Polly Plummer born.

1 Creation of Narnia. The Beasts made able to talk. Digory plants the Tree of Protection. The White Witch Jadis enters Narnia but flies into the far North. Frank I becomes King of Narnia

1900 Polly and Digory carried into Narnia by magic Rings.

180 Prince Col, younger son of King Frank V of Narnia, leads certain followers into Archenland (not then inhabited) and becomes first King of that country.

204 Certain outlaws from Archenland fly across the Southern desert and set up the new kingdom of Calormen.

1927 Peter Pevensie born.
1928 Susan Pevensie born.

300 The empire of Calormen spreads mightily. Calormenes colonize the land of Telmar to the West of Narnia.

1930 Edmund Pevensie born.

302 The Calormenes in Telmar behave very wickedly and Aslan turns them into dumb beasts. The country lies waste. King Gale of Narnia delivers the Lone Islands from a dragon and is made Emperor by their grateful inhabitants.

1932 Lucy Pevensie born.
1933 Eustace Scrubb and Jill Pole born.

407 Olvin of Archenland kills the Giant Pire.

460 Pirates from our world take possession of Telmar.

570 About this time lived Moonwood the Hare.

898 The White Witch Jadis returns into Narnia out of the far North.

900 The Long Winter begins.

1000 The Pevensies arrive in Narnia. The treachery of Edmund. The sacrifice of Aslan. The White Witch defeated and the Long Winter ended. Peter becomes High King of Narnia.

1940 The Pevensies, staying with Digory (now Professor) Kirke, reach Narnia through the Magic Wardrobe.

1014 King Peter carries out a successful raid on the Northern Giants. Queen Susan and King Edmund visit the Court of Calormen. King Lune of Archenland discovers his long-lost son Prince Cor and defeats a treacherous attack by Prince Rabadash of Calormen.

1015 The Pevensies hunt the White Stag and vanish out of Narnia.

1050 Ram the Great succeeds Cor as King of Archenland.

1502 About this time lived Queen Swanwhite of Narnia.

1998 The Telmarines invade and conquer Narnia. Caspian I becomes King of Narnia.

2290 Prince Caspian, son of Caspian IX, born. Caspian IX murdered by his brother Miraz who usurps the throne.

2303 Prince Caspian escapes from his uncle Miraz. Civil War in Narnia. By the aid of Aslan and of the Pevensies, whom Caspian summons with Queen Susan's Magic Horn, Miraz is defeated and killed. Caspian becomes King Caspian X of Narnia.

1941 The Pevensies again caught into Narnia by the blast of the Magic Horn.

2304 Caspian X defeats the Northern Giants.

2306–7 Caspian X's great voyage to the end of the World.

1942 Edmund, Lucy and Eustace reach Narnia again and take part in Caspian's voyage.

2310 Caspian X marries Ramandu's daughter.

2325 Prince Rilian born.

2345 The Queen is killed by a Serpent. Rilian disappears.

2356 Eustace and Jill appear in Narnia and rescue Prince Rilian. Death of Caspian X.

1942 Eustace and Jill, from Experiment House, are carried away into Narnia.

2534 Outbreak of outlaws in Lantern Waste. Towers built to guard that region.

1949 Serious accident on British Railways.

2555 Rebellion of Shift the Ape. King Tirian rescued by Eustace and Jill. Narnia in the hands of the Calormenes. The last battle. End of Narnia. End of the World.

A MAP OF NARNIA AND THE SURROUNDING COUNTRIES

INDEX

Numbers in *italics* refer to illustrations.

CLIVE STAPLES LEWIS was born in Belfast in 1898. He was sent to school in England, went on to Oxford University to read Classics and remained there as a Fellow and Tutor in English Literature. In 1954 he was made Professor of Medieval and Renaissance Literature at Cambridge University, a position he held until a few months before his death in 1963.

C. S. Lewis wrote books of literary criticism and on the Christian religion, as well as adult novels. *The Chronicles of Narnia*, his only novels for children, were written between 1949 and 1956 and have since become classics of children's literature.

PAULINE BAYNES was born in England but spent her early childhood in India. She returned to England and later studied art at the Slade School of Fine Art. In 1968 and 1972 she was winner and runner-up respectively of the prestigious Kate Greenaway Medal.

She was first commissioned to illustrate *The Lion, the Witch and the Wardrobe* in 1949 and went on to produce hundreds of wonderful illustrations for the seven chronicles of Narnia. The stunning new paintings for *A Book of Narnians* confirm her position as one of the foremost illustrators of children's books.

JAMES RIORDAN grew up in Portsmouth, England, and now works at the University of Surrey where he is Professor of Russian Studies and Academic Head of the Department of Linguistic and International studies.

Well-known for his collections of folktales from around the world, James Riordan has over thirty children's books to his credit and was winner of the prestigious Russian Peace Prize for his contribution to Russian folklore.